Weather Patterns

Jen Green

Published in paperback in 2014 by Wayland

Wayland
338 Euston Road
London NW1 3BH

Wayland Australia
Level 17/207 Kent Street
Sydney, NSW 2000

Senior editor: Camilla Lloyd
Designer: Simon Borrough
Consultant: Rob Bowden
Picture researcher: Shelley Noronha
Artwork: Ian Thompson
Sherlock Bones artwork: Richard Hook

Picture Acknowledgments: The author and publisher would like to thank the
following for allowing their pictures to be reproduced in this publication: Cover:
Getty Images; 1,20 Digital Vision/Getty Images, 4 Franck Guiziou/ Getty Images,
5 David Sutherland/Getty Images, 7 © Rob Howard/CORBIS. 8 © Ashley
Cooper/ Corbis, 9 © Bartosz Liszkowski/istock, 10(tl & bl) Digital Vision/Getty
Images, 10(br)Darryl Torckler/ Getty Images, 12 Digital Vision/Getty Images, 13
© George H.H. Huey/Corbis, 14 Getty Images, 15 Digital Vision/Getty Images,
17 © Tim Thompson/CORBIS, 18 © Leisa Johnson/Corbis, 20 Digital
Vision/Getty Images, 21 istock, 22 Getty Images, 23 istock, 24 National
Geographic/ Getty Images, 25 Getty Images, 26 © Warren Faidley/Corbis, 27
Dennis Hallinan/Alamy, 28 © Jim Reed/CORBIS, 29 © John Van Hasselt/Corbis.

British Library Cataloguing in Publication Data:
Green, Jen
  Weather patterns. - (The geography detective investigates)
  1. Weather - Juvenile literature 2. Climatology - Juvenile
  literature
  I. Title
  551.6

ISBN: 978 0 7502 8233 8

Printed in China

10 9 8 7 6 5 4 3 2 1

Wayland is a division of Hachette Children's Books, an Hachette UK company.
www.hachette.co.uk

Contents

Words that appear in **bold** can be found in the glossary on page 30.

The Geography Detective, Sherlock Bones, will help you learn all about Weather Patterns. The answers to Sherlock's questions can be found on page 31.

What are weather patterns?

The weather is the conditions in the **atmosphere** at a particular time – whether it is hot or cold, cloudy or sunny, dry or rainy, calm or windy. In some places the weather changes from day to day, and even from hour to hour. In other places it may stay the same for weeks on end.

All weather happens in the atmosphere – the thick layer of gases that surrounds our planet like a blanket. The atmosphere stretches 640 km (400 miles) into space. Weather happens in the lowest level of the atmosphere, called the **troposphere**. This layer extends 10-16 km (5.5-10 miles) above the surface. It contains the most air and also the most **moisture**. The gases in the atmosphere thin out as you move toward space.

Weather sometimes changes very quickly, as storm clouds move across a blue sky to shed rain.

Weather is not the same as **climate**. The weather is what is happening in the air at any given moment. The climate is the average weather patterns of a region, as measured over a long period – usually 30 years.

Weather affects our daily lives: the clothes we put on in the morning, how we travel, and even the food we eat. It affects whether crops do well. Long-term weather patterns affect where we build our homes and how we build. In recent years, the weather seems to be becoming wilder and less predictable, and storms, **droughts** and floods regularly hit the headlines. This book will explain what causes all the different types of weather, and how you can record local weather patterns.

DETECTIVE WORK

Think about weather patterns where you live. How does the weather change from day to day, and through the year? Find out about local weather records using a library or the Internet. You could try typing 'weather records' and the name of your region into a search engine.

These children in Vietnam, Southeast Asia are sheltering from the rain on their way to school.

What causes the weather and seasons?

The Sun provides the energy that creates the weather. The Sun's rays heat the land, oceans and air in different parts of the world by different amounts. This produces winds, clouds and other weather systems.

The Sun's rays travel in straight lines towards Earth. The curving surface of our planet means that they strike different parts of the Earth more or less directly, which affects their heating power.

In **tropical** regions around the **equator**, the Sun beats down from directly overhead. The Sun's rays strike Earth at right angles and are concentrated over a small area. This means the Tropics are always hot. Near the **poles**, Earth's surface curves away, and the rays strike less directly. They are spread over a larger area and also have further to travel through the atmosphere, which weakens their heating power. All this means the poles are always cold. **Temperate** regions in between generally have a more moderate climate – not too cold and not too hot.

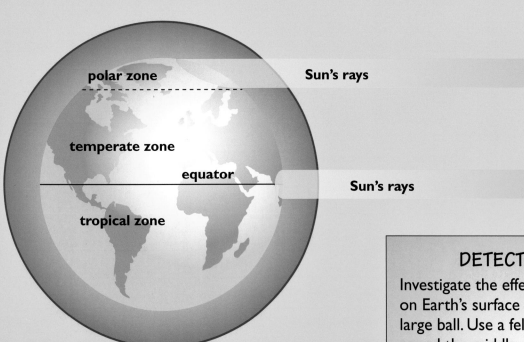

This diagram shows the effects of the Sun's rays on different parts of the Earth. The rays that reach the Earth near the equator contain more energy and heat.

DETECTIVE WORK

Investigate the effects of the Sun's rays on Earth's surface using a torch and a large ball. Use a felt tip to draw a line round the middle of the ball to represent the equator. Hold your torch at right angles to the 'equator'. You will see the torch lights a small area brightly. What happens when you move your torch up towards the 'poles'?

During the Arctic summer the Sun never dips below the horizon. That's why the poles are known as the 'lands of the midnight sun'.

In many parts of the Earth, weather patterns vary through the year. These changes are called the **seasons**, and they happen because our planet tilts on its **axis** as it circles the Sun. The tilt always points the same way in space. In summer the region where you live tilts towards the Sun, in winter it leans away. Temperate parts of the world have four seasons: spring, summer, autumn and winter. The Tropics always tilt towards the Sun so they don't have four seasons.

FOCUS ON

Polar seasons

The polar regions experience the greatest seasonal changes of any place on Earth. In summer each pole is bathed in sunlight, and it is light for 24 hours a day. In winter it tilts away from the Sun, and it is dark all day. Polar summers are cold and winters are bitterly cold!

Why do winds blow?

Winds are moving air masses. The Sun's heat sets the air in motion. Air heated by the Sun expands and becomes less dense – in other words, lighter. The warm air rises, and cooler air flows in to replace it. The movement of air produces a wind.

Strong winds by the sea in Cumbria, United Kingdom bend these hawthorn trees out of shape.

If you watch or listen to weather reports, you'll hear experts talking about areas of high and low **air pressure**. What exactly does this mean? Air pressure is the weight of all the air in the atmosphere pressing down on Earth. But the pressure is not the same everywhere. Where warm air rises, it creates a zone of low pressure, where air presses down less than elsewhere. Where cool air sinks, it creates a zone of high pressure. Winds blow as air moves from a high-pressure zone to a low-pressure zone, like air leaking out of a balloon.

Every part of the Earth has a regular wind pattern. The winds that blow most often are called **prevailing** winds. On either side of the equator, warm air rises and flows towards the poles. Later it cools, sinks and flows back toward the equator, completing the circle. The world's winds are bent by the planet's rotation. This is called the Coriolis Effect.

Study the photo of the tree on the opposite page. Can you tell the direction of the prevailing wind?

Sailing boats use energy from the wind to move across the ocean.

How do clouds, fog and dew form?

Clouds are floating masses of moisture. They are made up of billions of tiny water **droplets** or ice **crystals**. Clouds form when warm, moist air rises and cools, and the moisture turns to liquid droplets. This process is called **condensation**.

There are three main types of cloud. Cirrus clouds are high, wispy clouds made of ice crystals. Stratus are low-level grey clouds which may blanket the sky. Cumulus clouds are fluffy-looking. They are usually linked with warm weather. One type of cumulus, towering cumulonimbus clouds, produce thunderstorms.

DETECTIVE WORK

Study clouds over a few days. Sketch or photograph the different formations you see. Try to identify them using the photographs shown here.

These pictures show the three types of clouds, cirrus (left), cumulus (below left) and stratus (below).

Clouds play a major role in the water cycle – the endless circling of moisture between the land, oceans and air. As the Sun heats the land and particularly the ocean surface, moisture rises in the form of an invisible gas called **water vapour**. We call this **evaporation**. Later when the warm, moist air rises, moisture condenses to make clouds. When these shed rain, water seeps into the ground or drains away into rivers, which return the water to the oceans.

Clouds often form in places called weather **fronts** where cold and warm air masses meet. In a warm front, a mass of warm air slowly slides above cold air. Moisture condenses to form clouds which shed rain or **drizzle**. In a cold front, a mass of cold air burrows under warm air, which shoots upwards. Clouds, rain and sometimes storms result.

Fog and mist are basically clouds that have formed at ground level. When we can see less than 1 km (0.6 miles) through the cloud we call it fog. When we can see between 1 and 2 km (0.6-1.2 miles) we call it mist. Dew is another type of moisture. It forms at night when the ground loses heat quickly, and moisture condenses on cold surfaces such as grass.

This diagram shows how moisture circulates between the land, sea and air in the water cycle.

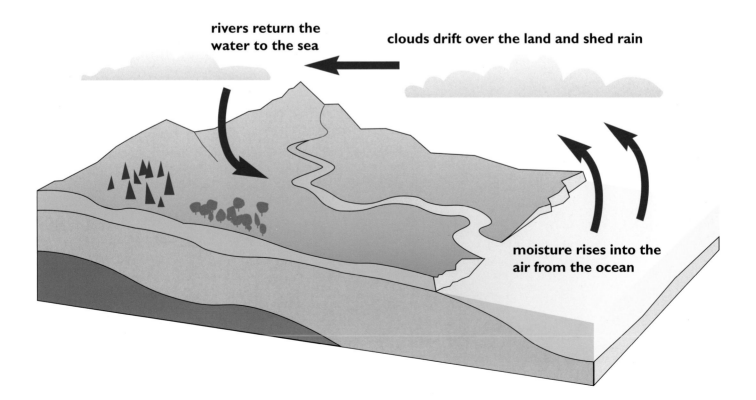

rivers return the water to the sea

clouds drift over the land and shed rain

moisture rises into the air from the ocean

Why does it rain?

The moisture that collects in clouds eventually falls from the sky as rain, **sleet**, snow or hail. Falling moisture is called **precipitation**. Rain and sleet are liquid precipitation. Snow and ice are moisture in solid form.

The billions of tiny water droplets in clouds float on rising air currents. When droplets collide they join to form bigger droplets. Eventually they get so heavy they fall to the ground. In cold clouds, ice crystals form snowflakes, which may melt on the way down to fall as rain.

Rain is vital to living things on Earth. It provides water for plants and animals, and collects in rivers and lakes to provide water for drinking, farming and industry. However the world's rainfall is not evenly distributed. Much of the Tropics and many coasts get heavy rainfall. Deserts may get almost no rain for years.

FOCUS ON

Monsoon rains

India, Southeast Asia and other tropical regions have a dry and rainy season. Changeable winds called **monsoons** blow in off the ocean at certain times of year, bringing heavy rain. At other times dry winds blow in the opposite direction. Monsoon rains provide much of the annual rainfall, up to 80 per cent of annual rainfall in some parts of India.

Wet monsoon winds water Kashmir in India in early summer. The annual drenching is vital to the region's crops.

Farmers depend on rain to water their crops, but rainfall patterns can be unreliable. Torrential rain can produce floods. In 1998, the Yangtze River in China burst its banks, killing over 3,500 people and destroying 5 million homes. If a cloudburst (heavy shower) hits a desert, rainwater floods dry gullies, forming temporary rivers. In mountainous areas, rivers can rise incredibly quickly and produce a sudden flood called a **flash flood**.

Water gushes down a dry stream bed, called a wadi, after a cloudburst in a desert.

DETECTIVE WORK

Measure local rainfall by making your own rain gauge. Cut a plastic bottle in half and put the top half upside-down inside the base to make a funnel. Tape a ruler to the side. Place the rain gauge in the open. If possible dig a shallow hole so it does not blow over. Empty the container once a week and note the amount of rain it holds.

Why do you think water spills off the land after a cloudburst in the desert?

How do snow, hail and frost form?

Snow, frost and hail are all types of frozen moisture. They form when the temperature falls below 0° Celsius (32° Fahrenheit) – the point at which water freezes to become ice.

High in the clouds, the air temperature is below freezing. Water droplets turn to ice crystals, which bump together and join to become bigger. Snowflakes form when ice crystals fall through clouds in certain conditions. If the ground temperature is just above freezing, the flakes partly melt on the way down, to form slushy sleet. In cold temperatures the snow settles on the ground, where wind may blow it into deep drifts.

Some of the snow that falls in the polar regions and on high mountains never melts. As more snow falls, the layers beneath get packed down to form ice. A thick cap of ice covers land in the polar regions, while icy **glaciers** flow slowly down from mountains.

If you cut a hailstone in two you can see layers of clear and cloudy ice inside. Clear layers formed near the base of the cloud where moisture froze slowly. Cloudy ice formed near the cloud top where moisture froze quickly.

Hail forms when ice crystals are tossed up and down inside storm clouds by swirling air currents. Each time the hailstone whirls up and down, new layers of ice are added. Eventually the stone gets so heavy it plummets downwards. Most hailstones are the size of peas or marbles, but really big ones are the size of golf balls. A shower of large hailstones can shatter glass and wreck fields of crops.

FOCUS ON

Frost forms in winter when water vapour condenses on cold surfaces such as leaves and window panes, and freezes instantly. The ice crystals form feathery patterns that look pretty, but a severe frost can kill crops and garden plants.

Can you explain exactly how the icicles in the picture formed?

Icicles hang off this building in the United States.

What is the weather like on coasts?

Places by the sea have a special weather pattern, called a **maritime climate**. Conditions are generally mild, but also windy. The weather is often wet because moist winds blowing off the ocean produce clouds that bring rain.

Coasts generally have a mild climate, with a smaller range of temperatures than places far inland. The sea influences temperatures in summer and winter, making them more even. This is because water warms up more slowly than the land, but also keeps its heat for longer. In summer, the oceans heat up slowly, cooling the land, but in winter the sea stays warm for longer, warming the coast.

In summer, coastal winds blow in opposite directions by day and night. By day, warm air rises above the land as it heats up quickly. Cool air flows in off the sea to replace it, creating what is called an onshore wind. At night the opposite happens. Cold air sinks over the land as it cools quickly. Cool air flows out to sea where air is still rising above the warm ocean. This creates a land (offshore) breeze.

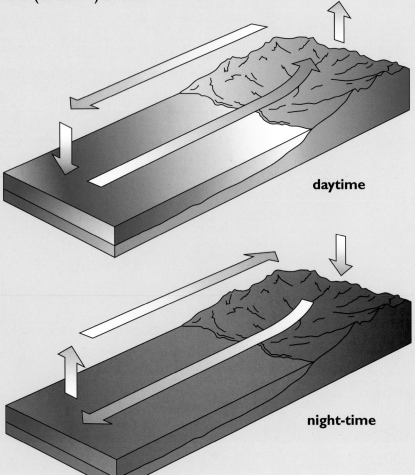

daytime

night-time

DETECTIVE WORK

Edinburgh in Britain lies at the same distance from the equator as Moskva (Moscow) in Russia. However Edinburgh lies close to the sea, while Moskva lies far inland. Compare temperatures in the two cities by typing their names into a climate website, for example www.worldclimate.com.

These diagrams show how winds change direction in summer on coasts.

Coastal weather patterns are also affected by warm or cold ocean currents flowing offshore. Warm currents flow from tropical seas, while cold currents flow from the polar oceans. The shores of western Europe are warmed by a warm current called the Gulf Stream. This begins in the Gulf of Mexico and flows across the Atlantic Ocean.

Can you explain how fog has formed in the picture below?

Fogs form at sea where warm, moist air flows above cold water. This happens off the coast of Newfoundland in eastern Canada.

FOCUS ON

Britain and Newfoundland in eastern Canada lie at about the same distance from the equator. However Britain's climate is several degrees warmer than that of Newfoundland. This is because the warm Gulf Stream swirls around Britain, whereas Newfoundland is cooled by a cold current flowing south from the Arctic.

Do mountains have special weather?

Like coasts, mountains have unusual weather patterns. The air high on mountains is 'thinner' or less dense than the air at sea level. Thin air holds less of the Sun's heat, so the temperature drops 1°C for every 150 metres (500 feet) you climb.

In cold temperatures snow falls instead of rain, and remains on rocky slopes instead of melting. That's why summits are usually snow-covered. High mountains have long, harsh winters and short, cool summers. They are also windy with changeable weather, often experiencing mist, sunshine, rain, snow and hail in a single day!

Snow is vital to one of the main industries in mountain regions: ski tourism. However heavy snow can make transport difficult. Mountain passes can be blocked by snow in winter. This can isolate remote villages. Most roads and railways keep to sheltered valleys, where towns and villages have grown up too.

Forests grow on the lower slopes of mountains. Higher slopes have grassy pastures, but conditions at the top are too harsh for plants to grow.

The Alpine town of Courmayeur stands at around 1,210 metres. It lies close to Mt Blanc, Europe's highest peak at 4,810 metres. If the summer daytime temperature on top of Mt Blanc is 6°C, what is the temperature in Courmayeur? Remember the temperature rises 1°C for every 150 metres you descend.

DETECTIVE WORK

Nairobi, Kenyatta in Kenya, Africa lies at around 1,624 metres (5328 feet). Mombasa in Kenya lies close to sea level. Compare temperatures in Nairobi, Kenyatta and Mombasa using a climate website on the Internet such as www.worldclimate.com.

Mountains have unusual rainfall patterns. Slopes facing moist winds blowing off the ocean receive high rainfall. As moist air rises up the mountain, the air cools and clouds form to bring rain. However the air has shed its moisture by the time it spills down the far side of the mountain. This creates a dry zone called a **rainshadow** on the far side.

This diagram shows the unusual rainfall patterns on mountains.

High, snowy slopes are at risk from **avalanches**. An avalanche occurs when a mass of snow breaks loose and thunders down the mountain. Avalanches can be triggered by high winds, a rise in temperature or even a loud noise. In August 2008, eleven climbers died on K2, the world's second-highest mountain, following an avalanche.

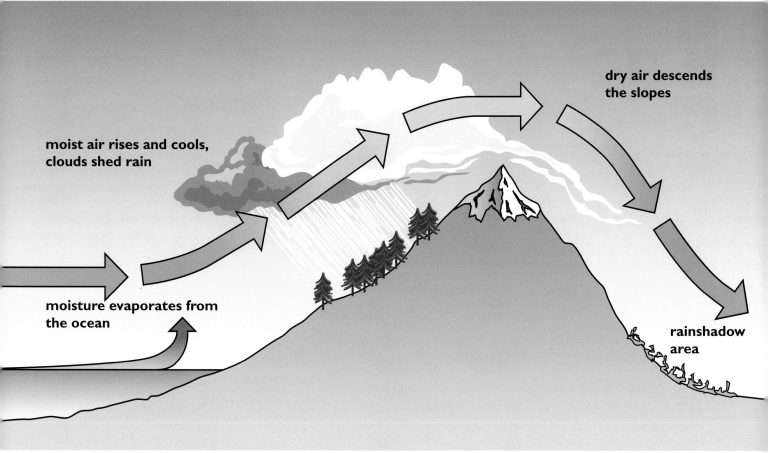

moist air rises and cools, clouds shed rain

dry air descends the slopes

moisture evaporates from the ocean

rainshadow area

What types of weather are dangerous?

Thunderstorms, **hurricanes** and **tornadoes** are extreme weather systems that can be dangerous. All three can produce very powerful winds and torrential rainfall, which can cause flooding. Hurricanes also produce extra-high tides when they sweep in from the sea.

Light travels so fast that you see a streak of lightning the instant it strikes.

Thunderstorms are created when powerful winds inside storm clouds cause water droplets and ice crystals to rub together. This causes electric charges to build up inside the cloud – positive charges at the top and negative charges at the bottom.

The charge is released when lightning sparks inside the cloud or down to the ground. The spark heats the air as it passes, creating a shock wave that we hear as thunder. Light travels much faster than sound, so you see lightning before you hear the thunder roll.

DETECTIVE WORK

In a thunderstorm, count the seconds between the lightning and thunder. The noise of thunder takes 3 seconds to cover 1 kilometre (5 seconds to cover 1 mile), so divide the number of seconds by 3 to work out the distance of the storm.

21

Hurricanes and tornadoes are violent spinning storms that form in hot, sticky weather. Hurricanes form out at sea. These huge storms can measure hundreds of kilometres across. Hurricane winds spin at up to 300 kph (185 mph) around a calm 'eye' in the centre. The eye sucks up water, creating a surge of water when the storm reaches land. In 2005, two-thirds of New Orleans in southern United States flooded when Hurricane Katrina hit the coast.

Tornadoes are also spinning storms, but they are much smaller than hurricanes and form on land. Hurricanes can rage for days, while tornadoes usually last only a few minutes. However the winds inside a tornado are even stronger than in a hurricane, spinning at up to 450 kph (280 mph).

Tornado danger

Tornadoes sometimes strike in groups called 'swarms'. In 1974, a total of 148 tornadoes ripped through the centre of the United States overnight, killing 330 people. Tornadoes are so common in the midwest of the United States that the area is nicknamed Tornado Alley. However, records show that the country with the greatest number of tornadoes recorded per square kilometre is Britain!

The dark, spinning funnel of a tornado reaches from a thundercloud to the ground.

How does weather affect us?

Around the world, people have learned to cope with all sorts of weather. Wearing the right clothing and living in houses suited to local conditions helps us to be comfortable. However weather hazards such as storms, drought and floods are beyond our control.

All over the world, houses are designed with the climate in mind. In hot countries, homes may have shutters to keep out strong sunlight, or be cooled by air conditioning. In cold places, houses have thick walls to keep in the warmth provided by fires or central heating. Windows may be double-glazed to keep out cold air. In dry regions, dwellings often have flat roofs, while in wet or snowy areas they have steep roofs to shed rain or snow. Along coasts and rivers where there is risk of flooding, houses are sometimes built on stilts.

FOCUS ON

Tornado danger

In the low-lying country of Bangladesh, farmers rely on seasonal rains to water their crops. If the rains fail, harvests are poor, but extra-heavy rains can bring flooding. In 2004, torrential rain caused local rivers to burst their banks. Floodwaters covered two-thirds of Bangladesh and 1,000 people died.

In 2004, torrential rain caused a flash flood in Boscastle, Cornwall. Cars were swept away by the flood.

A snowstorm hits New York City in the United States.

Weather also affects customs and the way we live. Daily temperatures help to decide when schools are open and the working hours of shops, banks and businesses. In southern Europe for example, people take a rest called a siesta in the afternoon to avoid the hottest time of day. Shops and offices close at lunchtime and open again when it's cool.

People who work outdoors are particularly affected by the weather. This includes builders and sailors. Farmers are especially dependant on the weather. They raise crops and rear animals that are suited to local conditions. However storms, floods and drought can all ruin harvests. When drought strikes a region, crops can wither and people can starve.

DETECTIVE WORK
Think about how the weather affects life where you live. How much time do people spend outdoors in winter and summer? Compare this with other countries you know of or have visited. Ask adults about the worst summer and winter weather they remember – and the best.

Is the weather changing?

Weather and climate don't stay the same forever, but slowly change over time. Throughout Earth's history, long, cold periods called **Ice Ages** have been been and gone. In between were warmer periods. The world has been slowly getting warmer since the last Ice Age ended 10,000 years ago.

In recent years, scientists have discovered that temperatures have started to rise more quickly. They believe that human activities are to blame. As factories, power stations, cars and planes burn oil, coal and gas for energy, they release air **pollution**. The waste gases are trapping more of the Sun's heat near the planet surface. This is called **global warming**.

No one can be sure how much warming there will be or how it will affect the weather. However many scientists believe that global warming is already making the weather unpredictable and wild. Storms, droughts and floods seem to be on the increase.

FOCUS ON

Greenhouse gases

Carbon dioxide, water vapour and other gases in the air form a layer that prevents some of the Sun's heat from escaping back into space. The gases act like the glass in a greenhouse, so they are called **greenhouse gases**. Scientists believe pollution from vehicles, power stations and factories is increasing natural levels of greenhouse gases in the air, which is producing faster warming of the Earth.

Scientists can find out about past climates by studying deep-level ice in Antarctica, which is thousands of years old. The ice holds a record of weather conditions when the snow fell.

Experts believe droughts like this one in a river basin in Australia are becoming more common due to global warming.

Ice in the polar regions is also starting to melt. If this trend continues, melting ice will swell the oceans, making sea levels rise. This would increase the risk of flooding on coasts.

What can be done about global warming? Scientists are calling on countries to reduce the amount of pollution they cause. But some countries are reluctant to act because they believe it will harm their economy. The good news is that we can all help to reduce the effects of global warming by using energy more carefully – for example, switching off lights and computers when they are not needed.

DETECTIVE WORK

Use your local library or climate websites to investigate how temperatures have risen in the last century. Type the name of your country and 'climate records' into a search engine, and see what you can find.

How do we predict the weather?

Knowing about the seasons gives us an idea of what weather to expect in spring, summer, autumn and winter. But if we need to know what the weather holds in detail, we consult the forecast. Weather predictions help us decide what clothes to wear, when and how to travel, and to plan outdoor activities such as sport.

Experts use information on weather systems all over the world to predict future weather. Weather stations on land, and ships and buoys at sea send **data** on temperatures, winds, clouds, rain and snowfall to international weather centres. More data comes from aircraft and weather balloons high in the air, and satellites orbiting in space. All this information is fed into very powerful computers that produce weather forecasts.

FOCUS ON

Weather warnings

Accurate weather forecasts can help to save lives. Weather experts issue warnings when severe storms and hurricanes are due. In September 2008, three years after Hurricane Katrina wrecked the city of New Orleans, experts warned another hurricane was approaching. As a safety measure, everyone left the city. In the event, the 2008 hurricane, named Gustav, was not as powerful as people had feared.

Satellites are used to track cloud systems and hurricanes as they travel across the face of the Earth. This image shows the progress of Hurricane Andrew as it swept across the Caribbean in 1992.

There are two main types of forecasts. Short-term forecasts provide a detailed picture of tomorrow's weather. Long-term forecasts paint a more general picture of weather over the next week or even month.

Weather forecasts are shown on maps using special symbols. As you know, air pressure (see pages 8-9) plays a big part in the weather. Weather maps often show areas of high and low pressure. High-pressure zones or 'highs' produce warm, sunny weather. Low-pressure zones or 'lows' often bring clouds and rain. Lines called **isobars** join up areas with the same air pressure. Where the isobars are close together, the weather will be windy. Warm and cold fronts (see pages 10-11) are also marked on weather maps.

DETECTIVE WORK

Weather forecasts are broadcast on TV, radio, the Internet and in newspapers. Compare weather forecasts for your area with the actual weather for a week. Were the forecasts accurate?

This map shows the weather forecast for North America. Warm fronts are shown with red semicircles; cold fronts are shown with blue triangles. Isobars are marked in green.

Study the weather map. What do you think the letters H and L stand for?

Your project

If you've done the detective work throughout the book and answered all of Sherlock's questions, you now know a lot about the weather! Use this information to produce your own weather project.

First you'll need to choose a subject that interests you. You could take one of these questions as a starting point.

Topic questions

• What is the weather like where you live? Start keeping your own weather records using your rain gauge and a thermometer. Note the temperature outdoors at the same time each day. Describe sunshine and wind conditions and record rainfall and cloud types. Compare your results to weather forecasts. Can you begin to predict the weather?

• Find out about weather patterns in different parts of the world. You could focus on a city or resort in the mountains and another by the coast, choosing two places in the same country or in different regions. Which gets the most rainfall? Which has the biggest range of temperatures throughout the year?

• Find out more about extreme weather patterns such as tornadoes, thunderstorms, floods and hurricanes. Some people drive long distances to see storms in action. They are called stormchasers, and some have their own websites.

These stormchasers are recording a thunderstorm in central United States.

Your local library and the Internet can provide all sorts of information. You could present your project in an interesting way, perhaps using one of the ideas below.

Sherlock has investigated how animals cope with extreme weather. He has found out that animals such as marmots cope with cold by hibernating (sleeping all winter). Many birds migrate (fly away) to avoid harsh weather.

Project presentation

- Draw or paste a map or maps of your chosen area in the middle of a large piece of paper. Add drawings or photos of all the different weather conditions experienced there around the map.

- In many parts of the world weather is important to tourism. Imagine you are writing a tourist brochure or making a TV documentary about how the weather affects life in the area. List the main points you want to put across and the people you might like to interview.

- Weather is very important to anyone that works outdoors, including sailors, fishermen, farmers, and people who run emergency services such as coastguard or the mountain rescue in the Alps. Imagine you are one of these people and write about how the weather affects your job throughout the year.

A mountain rescue team help an injured climber in the snow.

Glossary

air pressure The weight of all the air pressing down on Earth, pulled by gravity.

atmosphere The layer of gases which surrounds the Earth.

avalanche When masses of snow and rock break loose and slip down a mountain.

axis An imaginary line between the North and South Poles. The Earth spins on its axis.

carbon dioxide A gas in the atmosphere which traps the Sun's heat near the Earth.

climate The regular pattern of weather experienced in a region, as measured over several decades.

condensation When water changes from a gas into a liquid.

crystals Solid forms with regular shapes.

data Information.

drizzle Very fine rain.

droplets Tiny drops.

drought A period when no rain falls.

equator An imaginary line around the Earth's middle.

evaporation When water changes from a liquid into a gas.

flash flood When a river fills quickly after heavy rain, and bursts its banks.

front Region where warm air meets cold air.

glacier Mass of ice that slowly slides downhill.

global warming The warmer conditions that are being experienced worldwide, and that scientists believe are caused by a build-up of greenhouse gases.

greenhouse gases Gases in the air which trap some of the Sun's heat and so warm the Earth.

hurricane A huge spinning storm with very strong winds.

Ice Age Period in the past when the climate was colder than it is today.

isobars Lines on a weather map joining areas of equal air pressure.

maritime Belonging to the sea.

maritime climate The mild, wet climate that is typical on coasts.

moisture Wetness.

monsoon Changeable wind that bring rain at certain times of year.

poles The areas around the North and South Poles, also called the polar regions.

pollution Any solid, liquid or gas that harms nature.

precipitation When moisture falls from clouds as rain, sleet, snow or hail.

prevailing Of the main wind that blows in a region.

rainshadow A dry area located on the side of a mountain facing away from wet winds.

seasons Regular changes in weather and climate, that happen because Earth tilts as it travels through space.

sleet Slushy snow that has partly melted while falling.

temperate Of the zones between the Tropics and the polar regions, which have a mild climate.

temperature How hot or cold it is.

tornado Funnel of spinning air that form below a thundercloud.

tropical Of the region around the equator, called the Tropics, where the Sun is more directly overhead.

troposphere The lowest layer of the atmosphere.

water vapour Moisture in the form of a gas.

Answers

Page 9: A tree's leaves grow more strongly on the side facing away from the prevailing wind. The prevailing winds that have bent these trees blow from the right of the picture.

Page 13: Water pours off the land following a downpour in the desert because the ground is too dry to absorb the rain.

Page 15: Icicles start to form when the sun melts ice or snow, and water begins to drip down. In the cold air the dripping water refreezes to make a dagger of ice called an icicle.

Page 17: Fog forms where warm, moist air comes in contact with a cold sea surface, and cools quickly. The moisture condenses to form low cloud – fog.

Page 18: Courmayeur lies 3,600 m below the summit of Mont Blanc. The temperature rises 1°C for every 150 m you descend, so this height loss gives a temperature rise of 24°C. If the temperature at the top was 6°C, the temperature in Courmayeur is 30°C.

Page 27: 'H' stands for High – an area of high pressure. 'L' stands for Low – an area of low pressure.

Further information

Further reading
Weather and Climate by John Corn (Franklin Watts, 2004)

Earth's Changing Climate: Weather and Climate by Jim Pipe (Franklin Watts, 2004)

Nature Activities: Weather Watcher by John Woodward (Dorling Kindersley, 2006)

Earth Wise: Weather by Jim Pipe (Franklin Watts, 2008)

Our Earth in Action: Weather by Chris Oxlade (Franklin Watts, 2009)

Weatherwise: Rain and Floods by Patience Coster (Wayland, 2009)

Weatherwise: Snow and Blizzards by Robyn Hardyman (Wayland, 2009)

Weatherwise: Sunshine and Drought by Kate Purdie (Wayland, 2009)

Websites
BBC Weather
The BBC site on local and world weather.
www.bbc.co.uk/weather

Extreme weather
The US National Oceanic and Atmospheric Administration has details of extreme weather systems and global warming
www.noaa.gov/.

World climate
A website containing analysis of the climate of hundreds of towns and cities around the world
www.worldclimate.com.

Index

The numbers in **bold** refer to pictures